Heinemann History

Life & Work in 19th Century Britain

Depth Studies

Rachel Hamer

Heinemann Educational,
a division of Heinemann Publishers (Oxford) Ltd,
Halley Court, Jordan Hill, Oxford OX2 8EJ

OXFORD   LONDON   EDINBURGH   MADRID
ATHENS   BOLOGNA   PARIS   MELBOURNE
SYDNEY   AUCKLAND   SINGAPORE   TOKYO
IBADAN   NAIROBI   HARARE   GABORONE
PORTSMOUTH   NH (USA)

© Rachel Hamer 1995

The moral right of the proprietor has been asserted

First published 1995

95 96 97 98 10 9 8 7 6 5 4 3 2 1

British Library Cataloguing Data is available from the British Library on request.

ISBN 0 435 30929 3

Designed by Ron Kamen, Green Door Design Ltd, Basingstoke

Illustrated by Brian Kemp and Wayne Summers

Printed in Spain by Mateu Cromo

The front cover shows people waiting for help in the workhouse in a painting by Sir Luke Fildes (1874).

Acknowledgements

The author and publisher would like to thank the following for permission to reproduce photographs:

Bridgeman Art Gallery/Royal Holloway and Bedford New College: Cover
Elton Collection, Ironbridge Gorge Museum Trust: 4.1
Mary Evans Picture Library: 1.2, 2.12, 3.1, 3.2, 3.4, 3.7, 4.3, 4.4, 5.1
Her Majesty the Queen: 4.9
Hulton Deutsch Collection: 4.5
Ipswich Borough Museums and Galleries: 1.1
Lawrence and Wishart: map on page 14
Mansell Collection: 2.4, 2.7, 2.8, 2.9, 2.13, 3.3
Master and Fellows of Trinity College, Cambridge: 4.6
Sunderland Public Libraries, Museum and Art Gallery: Page 19

Every effort has been made to contact copyright holders of material published in this book. Any omissions will be rectified in subsequent printings if notice is given to the publisher.

Details of written sources

In some sources the wording or sentence structure has been simplified to ensure that the source is accessible.

G. Best, *Mid-Victorian Britain, 1851-75*, Weidenfeld and Nicolson, 1971: 5.4
William Cobbett, *Rural Rides*, Penguin, 1967: 2.6, 2.12
C. Culpin, *Making Modern Britain*, Collins Educational, 1987: 5.3
Frank Victor Dawes, *Not in front of the servants*, Century Hutchinson, 1989: 4.6
M.W. Flinn (ed.), *A Report on the Sanitary Conditions of the Labouring Class of Great Britain, 1842*, Edinburgh University Press, 1965: 2.12
Henry Mayhew, *London Labour and the London Poor, 1851*, Spring Books: 1.2, 4.7, 4.8
Peter Lane, *Batsford History Kits*, Batsford, 1975: 2.11
Peter and Mary Speed, *Working with Evidence: The Industrial Revolution*, Oxford University Press, 1985: 2.14
G.M. Young, *Victorian Essays*, Oxford University Press, 1962: 4.2

Note

In this book some of the words are printed in **bold** type. This indicates that the word is listed in the glossary on page 31. The glossary gives a brief explanation of words that may be new to you.

Contents

Unit 1	Changes in Britain 1750-1900: An Overview	4
Unit 2	What were the effects of the Industrial Revolution?	6
Unit 3	How did reform come about?	14
Unit 4	What were living standards like in the second half of the 19th century?	22
Unit 5	Was Britain a better place to live in 1900 than in 1750?	28
Glossary		31
Index		32

UNIT 1
Changes in Britain 1750–1900: An Overview

In 1750 most people in Britain lived in small villages. London, with a population of 500,000 people, was the only city of any size. The majority of people earned their living by farming in ways which had hardly changed since the Middle Ages.

There were few **factories**. Almost all the industries were on a small scale. Coal mines employed only a few miners and iron was smelted in clearings in the forests. The making of woollen cloth was the most important industry. This was usually carried out in people's homes with all the family joining in. This was known as the domestic system.

Between 1750 and 1900 the population of Britain grew very quickly. From eight million in 1750 it increased to 21 million in 1851. By 1900 it was 37 million.

This increase in population sparked off an increased demand for goods. British industry became based in large mechanized factories which were built on the coal fields. The machines were driven by steam engines. Around the factories grew large towns, as people moved from the countryside in search of work.

By 1851, Britain was the **'workshop of the world'**. The Great Exhibition was opened by Queen Victoria. It was held to celebrate the 'Works of Industry of All Nations' in the specially

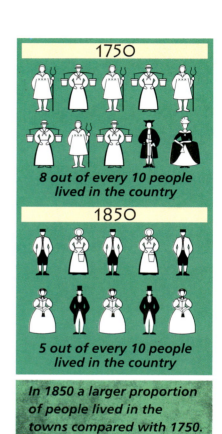

8 out of every 10 people lived in the country

5 out of every 10 people lived in the country

In 1850 a larger proportion of people lived in the towns compared with 1750.

SOURCE 1

The Suffolk village of East Bergholt painted by John Constable (1776–1837) in about 1812. Constable was a landscape painter. He lived for a time in East Bergholt.

4

SOURCE 2

'Under the Viaduct', an engraving of London, completed in 1872, by the French artist Gustave Doré (1833–83).

	1800	1900
Birmingham	71	760
Bradford	13	280
Liverpool	82	700
Manchester	75	645

Population growth in some British cities 1800 – 1900 (figures in thousands).

SOURCE 3

The people press, two and three deep, watching intently the operations of the moving machinery. Farmers with their mouths wide agape, lean over the bars to see the self-acting mules at work. They smile as they see the frame automatically draw itself out and run back in again.

Henry Mayhew, a social commentator and journalist, describing the interest in machinery at the Great Exhibition of 1851.

built Crystal Palace. Here, the six million people who came to the building in Hyde Park could see goods which were traded in all parts of the world.

The greatest inventions of the age were British. Britain produced more than half the world's cotton cloth. Iron foundries poured out more than half the world's pig iron. Britain had the largest merchant fleet which carried goods to the **British Empire** and the rest of the world.

For many people the changes were bewildering. The old certainties of village life began to disappear. The rapidly growing towns were never big enough to accommodate the numbers scrambling for house room. They were therefore overcrowded and lacked sanitation. In the face of a rising population, with the factories acting like magnets for those who needed jobs, the towns became dreadful places. Disease was always frightening and many people lived in squalid houses.

This book is about how these changes – often referred to as the **Industrial Revolution** – affected the living and working conditions of the people.

ACTIVITIES

1. Where did people live in Britain in 1750?
2. What changes took place between 1750 and 1900? Use statistics from the diagrams to support your answer.
3. How useful are Sources 1 and 2 as evidence of the changes which took place in Britain between 1750 and 1900?

What were the effects of the Industrial Revolution?

Working in the first factories

The cotton industry was the first to become factory-based. The first modern factory was founded in 1771 by Richard Arkwright at Cromford in Derbyshire. Here, the machines were powered by water. In 1780 Arkwright built the first cotton mill (factory) to be powered by a steam engine. Arkwright made large profits and other people soon followed his example. Edward Baines, writing in 1825 about Oldham in Lancashire, noted: 'Sixty years ago there was not a cotton mill in these parts; at present there are no fewer than 65.'

Factory discipline

The early factories were often dangerous, unhealthy and miserable places. The whole system was new, untried and unregulated. Working conditions varied greatly and improvements came only after many working people had experienced years of hardship and distress. Going 'out to work' was a completely new way of life. For factory owners it meant finding ways of organizing large numbers of people and making a profit. For employees it meant keeping to time and going out to work every weekday, instead of being at home. It also meant that for the first time the family was split up. Many factories had strict rules; those who broke them were punished. Workers were often heavily fined and the threat of dismissal was real. Both children and adults were beaten for making mistakes or falling asleep.

SOURCE 1

Area	1787	1835
Cheshire	8	109
Derbys	22	96
Lancs	41	683
Yorks	11	126
Scotland	19	159

The number of cotton factories in selected areas of Britain, 1787 and 1835.

SOURCE 2

NOTICE

List of Fines

For opening a window 1/-
For being dirty at work 1/-
For leaving an oil can out of place 1/-
For being five minutes after the bell 1/-
For having waste on the spindles 1/-
For whistling at work 1/-

A list of fines in a Manchester factory, 1840.

SOURCE 3

When my father introduced machinery into his own mill, the hours of labour were increased to twelve, for five days in the week, and eleven for Saturdays, making seventy one hours in the week. Other mill-owners, who used the same sort of machinery, worked their hands as much as eighty four hours a week.

John Fielden, a factory owner from Todmorden, Yorkshire, describing the long hours worked in the early factories.

SOURCE 4

Children in a spinning factory, 1830. Child labour was not new. It had been used under the domestic system. What was new was the dangerous machinery. Children swept under the unguarded machines whilst they were still in motion.

SOURCE 5

The task first given to him was to pick up the loose cotton that fell on the floor. He set to with diligence, although much terrified by the whirling motion and noise of the machinery, and half suffocated by the dust. Unused to the stench, he soon felt sick and his back ached with the constant bending. Blincoe, therefore, sat down. His task-master, Smith, told him that he must keep on his legs. He did so till twelve o' clock, being six and an half hours without rest. The moment the bell rang for dinner everyone rushed to get out of the mill as quickly as possible.

A description of Robert Blincoe's first day working in a cotton mill. It is taken from **A memoir of Robert Blincoe**, written by John Brown in 1828. Blincoe was seven years old.

SOURCE 6

In this room, which is lit from above, and in the most convenient and beautiful manner, there were 500 pairs of looms at work and 50 persons attending them. All the workers looked healthy and well dressed.

From William Cobbett, **Rural Rides**, 1830. This book was an account of a tour around England. Cobbett was a Radical – he wanted working-class people to have the vote. Here, he is describing John Fielden's factory.

Titus Salt

Not all factory owners treated their workers harshly. One business that really attracted the public eye was the great mill at Saltaire on the river Aire near Shipley, in Yorkshire, built by Sir Titus Salt. It was a model factory weaving mohair. Around the factory Salt built good quality housing for his workers. Sir Titus entertained 3,000 guests at a grand opening banquet, including over 2,000 workers brought by rail from his factory at Bradford. Such publicity and his prosperity helped to spread his ideas and encouraged others to follow his example. However, in a local paper *The Voice of the People*, he was nicknamed 'Tim Pepper' and mocked for his conceit in making his workers pay for a marble statue of himself.

QUESTIONS

1. What were working conditions like in many of the first factories?
2. Why were the rules so harsh?
3. Were conditions the same for all factory workers? Explain your answer.
4. How different was it working in a factory compared with working at home? Were any things the same?

SOURCE 7

Saltaire Mill in Yorkshire, a model weaving mill in the first model industrial town in Britain, founded in 1853 by Sir Titus Salt.

Living in the factory towns

Work in the factories began at 5.30 am. Everyone walked to work so they wanted to live as near to the factory as possible. Wages were low, so there was little money to spend on rent. It was essential to live as cheaply as possible. People moved into towns so rapidly and in such great numbers that there was not time to provide enough houses for them. Thousands of people were crowded into old or hastily built houses in the streets, or in closed courtyards near the factories.

Housing

For houses, as for factories, there were no laws to maintain standards. There were no effective safeguards to ensure a supply of clean water, proper drainage and sewerage, or to maintain the cleaning of the streets. The streets were not always paved. In the centre of the street was a gutter into which the dirty water from washing and cooking was poured. It often went stagnant and sometimes became clogged up with dead rats or rotting waste. The houses were grouped around a courtyard or in long terraces, often back to back. The **cesspit** was supposed to be emptied in buckets at night. When this was not done the sewage overflowed into the courtyard. Often the cesspit was next to the water pump which could cause contamination of the water. The smell was foul.

SOURCE 8

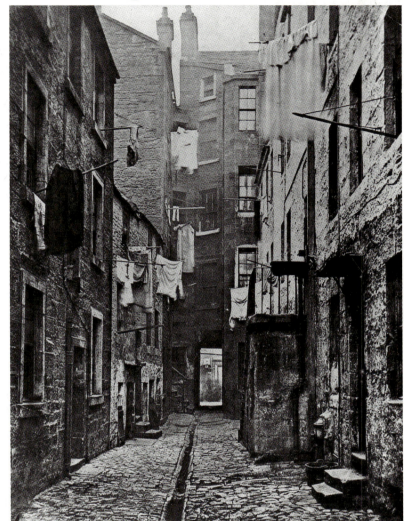

Close 75, High Street, Glasgow in 1868 – an example of overcrowded and insanitary conditions.

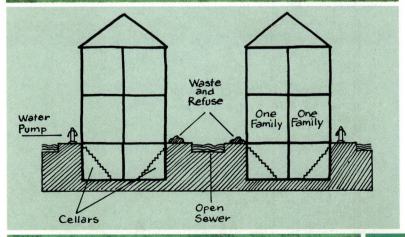

Back to back housing.

Cramped conditions

For most of the 19th century families could afford to rent only one room. The cheapest were cellars. They were usually very damp and had stone or earth floors. They had little light and were dark and cold. Rented rooms were generally not large enough for a whole family who had to cook, eat, wash and sleep in the limited space. There was a single grate for heat and cooking, with candles for light. In the summer it could be stifling as there was only one window and no through draught. Furniture was sparse. Living in this way, it was very difficult to keep clean and tidy. A few families, however, managed it (see Source 10).

The better-off lived in large houses on the outskirts of the town. They could afford to travel into the centre to work.

SOURCE 9

A Victorian family at home, living and dying in one room.

SOURCE 10

A poorer room, and yet a cleaner one I never saw; the table had been scoured until it shone again. There was a faded bit of carpeting on the floor and not a speck of dust from wall to wall. I have never seen a more striking instance of cleanliness taking away all the squalor of poverty.

*Taken from an article in **The Bradford Chronicle** in 1849. Bradford was a large industrial city, which produced woollen cloth. Workers lived in terraced back to back houses.*

THINK IT THROUGH

Look at Source 9. Think about all the difficulties of a family living in one room all the time. What would be hardest to put up with?

What does Source 12 tell us about Britain in the mid-19th century?

Diet

Cooking was very difficult. Bread was the staple food and was eaten with a scrape of butter or dripping or sometimes jam, with cups of tea for breakfast and tea. No plates or cooking utensils were needed for this, which made things easier. Boiled potatoes were the mainstay of dinner, with sometimes a little cheese, bacon or occasionally an egg. If there was meat on Sunday it was cooked in one pot with vegetables over the fire, or taken to a bakery to be cooked in an oven. There was little variety. Street sellers, such as piemen, sellers of hot green peas, eels, hot buns and puddings, helped to provide hot food if there was spare money to buy their wares.

Most families had to face disease. People accepted illness and early death as natural and normal. In the past there had been serious epidemics of plague or fever, but now that so many people were living together in one place infections such as cholera and typhus spread quickly and thousands of people died. The scale of such disasters was one reason which was, at last, to lead to improvements in public health and standards of building.

SOURCE 11

Butter (1½lb)	7p
Tea (1½oz)	2p
Bacon (1½lb)	4p
Milk (2 pints per day)	9p
Meat (1lb on Sundays)	3p
Potatoes	7p
Sugar	4p
Pepper, mustard and salt	1p
Soap and candles	7½p
Rent (per week)	17½p
Total	**62p**

A week's budget for a family of seven in Manchester in 1833.

SOURCE 12

The average age of death in 1842 in a town (Manchester) and a country area (Rutland). Taken from **A Report on the Sanitary Condition of the Labouring Class** by Edwin Chadwick (1800–90), a civil servant, who worked on the improvement of the **Poor Laws** and public health legislation. His report was published in 1842.

	Gentry	Farmers/Traders	Labourers
Rutland	52	41	38
Manchester	38	20	17

Mining villages

Not all workers lived in towns and cities. Many lived in agricultural or industrial villages, like the mining villages in such areas as Northumberland, Durham, the Midlands and South Wales. These were close-knit communities, sharing in a common danger. The demand for coal increased rapidly. More and more coal was needed to power machines, for railways and later, steamships.

Pit work was hard and dangerous. Men, women and children were employed for up to twelve hours a day. **Hewers** dug out the coal, their work lit by three or four candles. The hurriers dragged the cut coal in small trucks. It was taken to the surface on hoists or carried in **corves** up ladders or steep passages. Small children, as young as five, were employed as trappers. As trucks came along their job was to open and close the wooden doors which were installed in the passage ways to ventilate the mine.

SOURCE 14

Cause of death	Age		
	Under 13	13 – 18	Over 18
Fell down shaft	14	16	36
Drawn over pulley	3	–	3
Fall of stones or coal	15	14	72
Drowned	3	4	15
Explosion of gas	13	18	49
Suffocated	–	2	6
By tram waggons	4	5	12

The main causes of deaths in British coalmines, 1838.

SOURCE 13

Colliers' cottages, 1844. Inside the floors were beaten earth. They were dimly lit. Many smelt of 'human impurities'.

There were many threats to health. Not only was there the danger of explosion or pit falls, but the air was heavy with floating coal dust and smelled foul from the gases found underground. Although the new steam pumps helped to reduce the water in the mines, flooding was still a problem.

Agricultural villages

Agricultural labourers still formed the largest single group of workers in the early 19th century. Apart from ploughmen, shepherds and waggoners, labourers had to do whatever jobs the season required. In general, wages were lower than those of factory workers or miners. Wages were also higher in the north of England than the south.

All the family worked when they could, to make a living wage for everyone. For example, the youngest children scared away crows; there were turnips to drag and clean and **gleaning** to be done after the harvest.

Even so, farm workers in many parts of England were very poor. Their **tied cottages** were often no more than a single room with a lean-to for animals and as damp and smelly as any factory worker's room. New machinery, especially the threshing machine, meant that fewer labourers were needed. The rising population made the situation worse. There was not enough work on the farms. There was also no longer a need for hand-woven woollen cloth which could supplement wages. In the north of England, this situation was helped by the existence of alternative work in the factories, mines and iron works. In southern England there was serious unemployment which led to the Swing Riots of 1830.

SOURCE 15

A young boy scaring crows. All the family needed to work to make a living wage.

SOURCE 16

Many labourers do not have jobs. Instead they are employed by the parish digging and breaking stones for the roads. Yesterday I saw three poor fellows digging stones, who told me that they never had anything but bread to eat, and water to wash it down. One of them was a widower with three children and his pay was eighteen pence per day. Just such was the state of things in France at the eve of the **French Revolution**.

From Rural Rides by William Cobbett, 17 April 1830.

ACTIVITIES

1. What were living and working conditions like in (a) the towns and (b) the countryside?

2. Look back over the whole unit. Was it better living in a village in the country or in a town? Explain your answer.

UNIT 3

How did reform come about?

The reform of working conditions

For most working people, the Industrial Revolution meant long hours, low wages and poor housing. Sometimes **trade depressions** brought high unemployment and further hardship. To begin with nothing was done to help working people. Why did it take so long for the **reform** of working conditions to come about?

The Luddites

Without the right to vote or **combine** together, the only way for working people to make their discontent known was to present petitions or even turn to violence.

In 1811–12, many textile workers in Yorkshire, Lancashire, Nottinghamshire and Cheshire were thrown out of work by a trade depression. They blamed their plight on the introduction of machinery. Workers angrily smashed up machinery. These workers took their name from an invented character called Ned Ludd, and were known as Luddites.

The Swing Riots

In 1830 after a series of bad harvests, food prices went up. The farm labourers were also angry at the introduction of steam-driven threshing machines which threatened their jobs. Workers, led by a Captain Swing, an invented character, broke threshing machines and burnt haystacks.

The authorities were alarmed at these outbreaks of violence. They were afraid of a revolution taking place in England, like the one which had occurred in France in 1789. Instead of helping the workers, they punished them.

Early attempts to form trade unions

Some workers tried to help themselves by combining together. At first, these groups were called friendly societies and they helped fellow-workers to find jobs. They also gave out sick pay and funded funerals.

SOURCE 1

A cartoon from the time, portraying the Swing Riots. Do you think the cartoonist is sympathetic to the labourers?

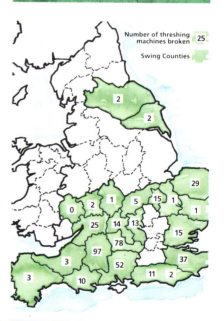

Counties in England where farm labourers rioted in 1830.

Attempts were made to form trades unions, which aimed to protect jobs, cut working hours and increase safety and wages.

In 1833, a number of unions joined together to form the Grand National Consolidated Trades Union (GNCTU). In 1834 six farm workers from the Dorset village of Tolpuddle were prosecuted for swearing an oath to form a local branch of the GNCTU. They were sentenced to transportation to Australia. Their harsh treatment put many workers off joining a union and the GNCTU collapsed.

What was needed was some direct link to Parliament where laws were made and could be changed.

Laissez-faire

Persuading Parliament that reforms were needed proved to be difficult. Why was this?

- Working people did not have the right to vote in the early 19th century.
- Most Members of Parliament were landowners and farmers from the south of England. They were not really interested in the problems of working people. Many had no knowledge of the northern textile mills.
- Most people believed that it was not the job of the government to interfere in people's lives; this belief was called *laissez-faire*.

The Ten Hours Movement

Two Factory Acts, passed in 1802 and 1819, were ineffective. In 1831 textile workers began campaigning for working hours to be limited to ten per day. There was a small number of MPs who were factory owners and supported shorter hours. They took up the cause. Michael Sadler, a linen manufacturer, became the leader of the Ten Hours Movement in Parliament. Most MPs, however, agreed with the argument that child labour and long hours were needed for the factories to make a profit.

Althorp's Factory Act 1833

- Young people, aged 9-13, to work no more than 48 hours per week, plus 2 hours schooling per day.
- No children under 9 to work in a textile factory.
- People, aged 13-18, to work no more than 69 hours per week.
- People under 18 not to work at night.
- 1½ hours per day for meal breaks.
- Four inspectors to enforce the law.

The terms of Althorp's Factory Act, 1833.

In 1832 the Earl of Shaftesbury became the leader of the Ten Hours Movement. He seemed to be an unlikely champion of the factory workers, as he came from a wealthy farming background. Shaftesbury, however, was a sincere and caring Christian. When he read reports in *The Times* about the conditions in factories, he was convinced that it was his duty to help. Parliament was pressured into setting up a commission to investigate conditions in the textile factories. The commission's report produced a mass of evidence which led to the passing of Althorp's Factory Act in 1833 (see above).

The 1833 Act did not alter conditions for many working men, women and children. It applied only to textile mills. Shaftesbury was disappointed that the Act had not achieved the ten hour day. It was important, however, because it was a first step towards the government accepting responsibility for decent working conditions. The belief in *laissez-faire* began to weaken.

The Collieries Act 1842

Shaftesbury continued the fight. In 1840 he persuaded the government to set up a Royal Commission to investigate conditions in the coal mines. Source 2 shows Shaftesbury visiting a mine as part of this campaign. The commission's report was published in 1842. It was graphically illustrated by artists who had been underground. The nation was shocked at the appalling conditions in which children and women worked. The Collieries Act of 1842 stopped boys under ten and women and girls from working underground in the mines. It also said that mining inspectors were to be appointed. Many women, however, were annoyed about the Act because it stopped them earning money.

Further legislation

Further factory acts followed (see page 17). In the last quarter of the 19th century half-day working on Saturdays and Bank Holidays began and inspectors checked all workplaces with machinery for manufacturing. Despite these improvements, there was still no insurance for workers. Unless workers belonged to a friendly society or a trade union, they received no money if they were absent from work.

SOURCE 3

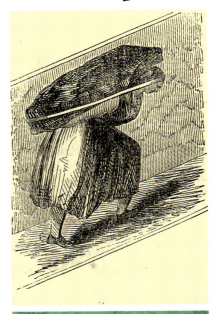

Women coal bearers in Scotland, from the **Mines Report, 1842**.

SOURCE 2

Anthony Ashley Cooper (1801–85), 7th Earl of Shaftesbury visits a mine, taken from the **Mines Report**, 1842. The boy in the picture worked as a hurrier.

FACTORY ACTS AFTER 1844

1844
Graham's Act
- No child under 8 years to work in a textile factory.
- A maximum 6½ hour day, with a half day at school for 8 – 13 year olds.
- Machinery to be guarded.

1847
Fielden's Ten Hours Act
- A maximum 10 hour day for women and children in textile factories. [Nothing said about the hours of men].

"We can get round this!"

"Easy! We'll work a shift system with the children. The men will work all the time and we'll keep the machines running!"

1850
Grey's Act
- Maximum working day for women and young people to be 10½ hours.
- Factories can be open only from 6.00 am to 6.00 pm.

Other laws passed
1867 All previous laws about textile factories to apply to all factories with more than 50 workers.

1874 Maximum week of 56½ hours for all factory workers.

1878 All workshops using machines to obey factory laws. Inspectors to check all factories and workshops.

Workers still not covered

Domestic servants   **Seamstresses**   **Shopworkers**   **Farm labourers**

QUESTIONS

1. Why did working people sometimes turn to rioting?
2. Why did Parliament not reform working conditions to begin with?
3. What was the Ten Hours Movement?
4. Why did the Earl of Shaftesbury get involved in factory reform?
5. How effective was the 1833 Factory Act?
6. Look at Sources 2 and 3. Why did such drawings make an impact on the public?
7. a What did the Collieries Act of 1842 say?
   b Why were some workers angered by it?
8. Which groups of workers were covered by these new laws and which were not?

The reform of living conditions

It proved even more difficult to get laws passed to improve the standard of housing and the water supply for the poor. The government was unwilling to do anything to improve matters. Besides, who was going to pay for the improvements? The local tax, or rate, was paid only by house owners. They lived in the better houses where there were better living conditions anyway. Why should they pay higher taxes to help others?

Progress came slowly. In 1835 the Municipal Corporations Act set up councils in all the main towns. Councils were given the powers, if they wished, to raise money for such things as paving the streets or putting in gas lights, but not much had been achieved.

Enter Edwin Chadwick

Chadwick's interest in people's health had grown when he was investigating the Poor Laws between 1832 and 1834. He thought that if he could show that foul living conditions caused disease, it would make the government realize that it cost less to prevent people getting ill than to pay to look after them when they could not work. In 1838 he got permission for a special survey of the conditions of the labouring classes in east London. The shocking findings of the report led to Chadwick's friend, the Bishop of London, proposing a report on all the cities in the country. *The Report on the Sanitary Condition of the Labouring Class* was completed in 1842 and became a best seller! It established that where there was no drainage, poor water supply and overcrowding there would be sickness and early death. This fact helped to challenge the views of many middle-class people that the way the poor lived was due to lack of effort on their part and that it was not the duty of the government to keep the people healthy. However, even a Royal Commission in 1844 confirming these findings still did not lead to real change.

The 1848 Public Health Act

Following an outbreak of cholera in 1848, Parliament passed the first Public Health Act. This set up a central Board of Health in London. The Act said that towns could set up their own local Board of Health if ten per cent of the ratepayers demanded it, or if the death rate was higher than 23 people per 1,000 in a year. The Act was not compulsory and many towns did not bother to follow it. The cholera outbreak passed away and interest in public health disappeared for a time.

SOURCE 4

Edwin Chadwick worked to improve public health.

SOURCE 5

There is nothing a man hates so much as being cleaned against his will, or having his floors swept, his walls whitewashed, his pet dung heaps cleaned away, all at the command of a sort of sanitary policeman.

*An extract from **The Times**, 1 August 1854. Many people strongly believed that cleanliness was nothing to do with the government.*

THINK IT THROUGH

How might cholera have spread to the better districts?

Disease

The most feared disease was cholera, which first struck Britain in 1831. It caused the death of thousands. There were further serious outbreaks in 1848, 1854 and 1866. It was a terrible disease which resulted in fever, sickness and diarrhoea. Death usually followed. Although it mostly affected the overcrowded and insanitary tenements of the cities, middle-class families also suffered. Pressure for change began to grow as a result. In 1854 Dr John Snow carried out some research in Soho, London. He was able to prove that cholera was carried in contaminated water. Then, in 1865, Louis Pasteur, a French chemist, showed that germs caused decay; there was a firm connection between dirt and disease. People began to realize that towns would have to be cleaned up.

Power to the people

In 1867 the vote was given to all male householders in the towns. Until then only the upper-class males had been able to vote. Working-class people at last had a direct influence on Members of Parliament. Now MPs had to listen to those who lived in the cities.

The 1875 Public Health Act

Finally, in 1875, Parliament passed a Public Health Act which drew together previous Acts. It made all town councils build effective sewers and provide a clean water supply and a Medical Officer of Health to organize and inspect the work. This time the measures were compulsory.

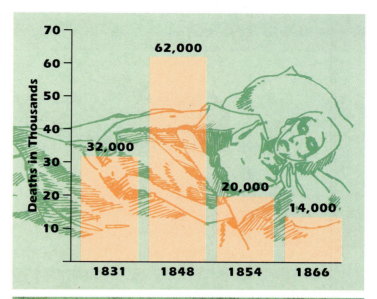

Deaths from cholera, 1831–66.

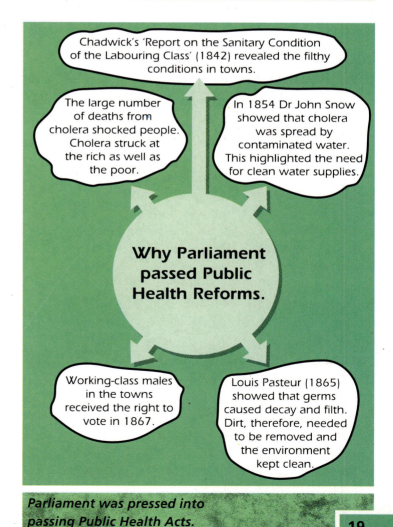

Parliament was pressed into passing Public Health Acts.

SOURCE 6

A row of terraced workers' houses built in the late 19th century. The problem was that not enough of these houses were built.

Improvements in housing – town councils

Parliament also introduced building regulations to improve the standard of housing. The Artisans' Dwelling Act (1875) gave town councils the power to knock down slums. They were also given the power to build new houses on the cleared ground or sell the land to private builders. Joseph Chamberlain, the lord mayor of Birmingham, took advantage of this Act and rebuilt the centre of the city. However, the Act was not a total success. Sometimes councils knocked down slums but did not build new houses to replace them. Private builders who built new houses on land bought from councils, usually charged such high rents that poorer people could not afford them.

Improvements in housing – private individuals

A number of individuals did important work to improve housing in the second half of the 19th century.

- In 1862 George Peabody, an American, gave a large sum of money for new workers' houses to be built in London.

- By 1871 Saltaire, built by Titus Salt (see page 8) had 800 houses, public baths, churches, shops and a park.

- Octavia Hill (1838–1912) borrowed money from rich friends and bought workers' houses to improve them. She then rented them out at a fair rent and still made a profit. She provided an example for other landlords to follow.

- In 1888 William Lever built Port Sunlight for his workers, and George Cadbury built the village of Bournville for his workers in 1895.

Despite these improvements, however, there were still many people living in cramped back to back houses.

Food and Drink

In the early 19th century factory workers were paid in tokens under the truck system. The only place the tokens could be spent was in the factory-owner's shop! The food here was often costly and had been tampered with (see Source 7). Favourite tricks in many shops were putting chalk in the flour and salt in the beer.

The Co-operative Movement

In 1844, a group of Rochdale weavers paid £1 each to open a shop in Toad Lane. Here they sold pure food at a fair price. If you bought goods at the shop you became a member and received a share of the profits (the dividend). The idea was so succesful that, by 1850, there were over 100 similar shops in the north of England. This was the start of the Co-operative Movement, which is still going today.

In 1871 a law was passed which made it illegal to pay workers in tokens. The Sale of Food and Drugs Act (1875) appointed shop inspectors to make sure that food was pure and shops clean.

SOURCE 7

'How food and drink were made!' – a cartoon from 1845, by George Cruikshank. What does it say about the production of food and drink?

ACTIVITIES

1. Why was reform in living conditions so slow in coming? You should think about:
    - *laissez-faire*
    - who had the right to vote
    - opponents of change.

2. Why did Parliament eventually step in to improve conditions? You should think about:
    - individuals who campaigned for reform
    - evidence of reports
    - who had the right to vote
    - disease.

3. What improvements were made in
    a housing
    b food and drink?

UNIT 4

What were living standards like in the second half of the 19th century?

Despite Parliament passing legislation to improve housing, public health and working conditions, the standard of living still varied greatly.

Skilled workers

It seems that people with a regular and secure job adapted better to the rapid industrial changes which had been taking place. About one-tenth of the working population were skilled **artisans**. Their wages were twice those of a factory worker and their conditions of work much better. The key to their relatively favoured position was often a long **apprenticeship** when they learnt their skills. From 1851 many skilled workers were able to join a trade union, which fought to protect members' jobs, raise wages and improve working conditions. Printers, jewellers, instrument workers, engineers, shipwrights and carpenters were all organized into trade unions. Workers in the newer trades such as fine cotton spinners, calico printers and dyers could afford to rent better houses and own many comforts. Unskilled workers, however, did not have any trade unions to join.

SOURCE 1

A union membership certificate of the Amalgamated Society of Engineers, a trade union for skilled workers, formed in 1851.

SOURCE 2

We will take a printer, a skilled man in good employ – 58 hours a week and a half holiday on Saturday. He travels to work by horse-drawn bus, wearing a morning coat and tall hat. He takes his midday meal at a chop house – a plate of veal and ham and a pint of good beer, one shilling [5p]. The father has a vote. The children, you may be sure, go regularly to school; on Saturday afternoon the family take a steamer to Greenwich or Gravesend. Sunday morning they all go to church or chapel while the joint is cooking in the baker's shop and in the afternoon they walk in the park and have their friends to tea. Their annual fortnight will be spent at Margate, if they want to be jolly.

A description of late Victorian England by an historian, G. M. Young, who began his life in the last twenty years of Queen Victoria's reign.

SOURCE 3

The Salvation Army serving hot stew to the poor at the Conder Street Mission Hall, London, in 1881. Many people still had to rely on charity.

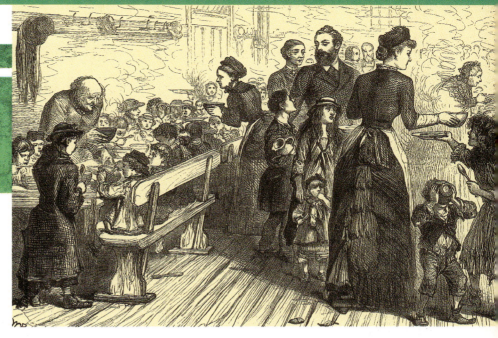

Unskilled workers

There were many sorts of labouring jobs in the ports and cities. These included dockers and dragmen, hodmen, builders, porters and coal backers. None of these jobs had any security. Workers were paid by the day or perhaps the week. In good years they might be employed for most of the year, but this might depend on their age, their health or even the weather. In times of depression work was hard to find; only the young and strong were likely to be hired.

In the 1880s trade unions for unskilled workers were formed. In 1889 the London dockers went on strike and won an increase in wages from the employers. Trade union membership began to rise.

For those ordinary families too poor to save it did not take much to bring disaster. There was very real fear of becoming ill for any length of time; or getting injured at work; losing a job or simply becoming too old and infirm to work any more. There was no National Insurance scheme and no old age pension. For many people there was no safety net other than the dreaded **workhouse**.

In the last years of the 19th century reports by Charles Booth in London and Seebohm Rowntree in York were published which provided evidence that, not only the elderly and those without work led miserable lives, but that many unskilled workers were paid such low wages that they could not afford the bare necessities of life. People like this probably numbered one-third of the population in these two cities. There was pressure for even more change after 1900.

Education

In the early 19th century schools for working-class children were provided by voluntary bodies. In 1870 Forster's Education Act introduced Board Schools for children aged 5–12. These schools were financed by the local rates and government grants; they provided a basic grounding in the **3Rs**. By 1899 elementary schooling to the age of 12 was free and compulsory. Pressure was growing for improved standards, and opportunities for secondary education were set out in the important Education Act of 1902.

THINK IT THROUGH

Why was educational opportunity so important to the working class?

The middle classes

The growing middle classes had far more security and lived much more comfortable lives. People in this section of society were identified by the 1841 **census** as

- independent persons (people with a private income).
- people in the professions (doctors, lawyers and teachers).
- government officers, people in the army, navy and civil service.

By the late 19th century the middle classes were more important than they had ever been before. They were defined by their greater income, which was expected to increase through life. However, within the middle class there was a big difference between the wealth of a successful factory owner and smaller merchants, shopkeepers or master tailors; between lawyers and clerks or schoolteachers. But they all described themselves as respectable people who did not earn their living by manual labour.

SOURCE 4

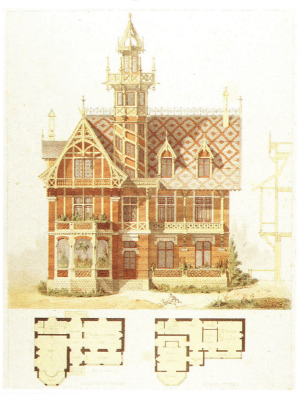

Middle-class housing in the late 19th century. Such detached houses were built on the edge of towns.

SOURCE 5

An upper middle-class Victorian living room.

Their income allowed them to rent or buy a comfortable home in a favourable area. For the lower middle class this might mean a terraced house with three bedrooms and three living rooms. Inside there was an increasing emphasis on comfort and decor. For those who could afford it, a kitchen, dining room, drawing room, library and three family bedrooms were desirable; plus a nursery and two servants' rooms.

Food was an important part of the budget. Entertaining for a well-off family was expensive. Many middle-class people travelled to work as they lived away from the town centre in the suburbs. Some owned carriages, but they were expensive to maintain. Most took a cab or, later, went to work by train. Clothes, too, were expensive as it was considered necessary to keep up with the fashion of the day.

Domestic servants

More than a million people at this time worked as domestic servants. In middle-class houses, except the very largest which had very large staffs, there would usually be three female servants. They would consist of a cook/housekeeper, a parlour maid and a 'tweeny' who did the rough work. Sometimes a manservant would be employed, perhaps to look after the horses or to act as butler and be in charge of the wine cellar. Even the least well-off people would employ one servant to come in each day.

For most of the year the servants' working day began before 6 am, when they lit the fires before breakfast, and ended when the warming pans had been put in the beds at night. No allowance was made if the servants had to wait up because the master and mistress were entertaining or out. In the early years of the 19th century there was no time off except to go to church. However, by the end of the century one day off a month was allowed.

SOURCE 6

Daily duties
Be downstairs at 6.30 am in the summer and 6.15 am in the winter.
Open shutters first.
Do dining room fire and dust room.
Lay breakfast by 8.15 am.
Dust hall and stairs, morning room and drawing room.
Clear dining room of breakfast dishes.
Make beds.
Answer the door, wait at meals, clear and wash up. Bring in coal as needed.

Weekly jobs
Mon: Wash glass and silver.
Tues: Clean dining room silver.
Wed: Clean hall and polish brass.
Thurs: Polish silver.
Fri: Clean pantry.
Sat: Dust dining room.
Sun: Lay afternoon tea and wash up.

*From **Not in front of the Servants**.*

Many of the servants worked in service from about the age of ten. It must have been hard to work away from home, with little time to visit the family. There was no legal protection for this large group of the working class, the majority of whom were women.

Everything depended on the goodwill or otherwise of the master or the mistress. Even the best employers regarded servants as belonging to them; some even changed their names if they happened to be the same as one of the family. Mary or Jane were names commonly chosen for them. Rarely did employers take an interest in servants as people. The most important thing was that servants should not get above themselves. But to some extent it was a sheltered and secure life. A servant could be sacked for laziness or being dishonest; but as long as they 'knew their place' and did their work thoroughly, they could be sure of a roof over their heads.

Entertainment for all

The reduction in working hours meant there was more leisure time for most people in the latter years of the 19th century. Wages had also improved for many workers. From 1875 there was also a fall in the cost of living, especially in food prices. All this meant there was a little more money for leisure and entertainment.

Most towns had a theatre where travelling companies performed. The larger cities had music halls where singers and circus acts, conjurors, and even performing animals, entertained the audience. The songs they sang became very popular and were sung at home or in public houses. There were penny concerts and street entertainers, Punch and Judy shows, clowns, peep-shows, street reciters, singers and barrel organs. 'Twopenny hops' were popular with the better-off workers (see Source 7). The circus was also a favourite with all audiences.

For the poorest, who could not afford to buy enough food, let alone a theatre ticket, or even travel on the railway, a penny was enough to get drunk and forget the hard work and troubles of the day.

The middle classes had always had more leisure time, but now more and more people were able to enjoy themselves in new pastimes such as cycling, tennis, hockey or golf. In 1873 the County Cricket Championship began, followed by the first Test Match in 1880. The FA Cup was first played for in 1878 and the Football League began in 1888, with Preston North End the first winners.

As means of transport began to improve, people were able to go further afield and no longer needed to rely on local

SOURCE 7

The numbers present at 'twopenny hops' vary from 30 to 100 of both sexes, their ages being from 15 to 45. At these there is nothing of the leisurely style of dancing, but vigorous, laborious capering.

Henry Mayhew in London's Labour and London Poor, 1851.

SOURCE 8

Love and murder suits us best, sir; but within these few years I think there is a great deal more liking for tragedies among us. They set a man thinking; but then we all consider them too long. Macbeth would be better liked if it was only the witches and the fighting.

We are fond of music. Sailor songs and patriotic songs are liked. A song to take hold of us most has a good chorus. The chorus of 'Britons never shall be slaves' is often rendered 'Britain always shall be slaves'.

A Londoner, speaking to Henry Mayhew. He is describing the ordinary person's taste in entertainment in 1851.

SOURCE 9

Ramsgate Sands in Kent, a popular seaside resort, painted by William Powell Frith in 1851-3. The railways made it possible for people to visit the seaside on cheap day excursions.

entertainments. They could now go for excursions by train and river steamers or get easily from one part of town to another by omnibus. This greatly contributed to the richness of people's lives.

In the 18th century the upper classes had discovered the pleasures of the seaside. Now the railways enabled working people to take a trip to such resorts as Blackpool, Clacton and Scarborough. Day-trippers went in large numbers and soon piers and promenades were being built for their entertainment. Later, boarding houses were opened for people to stay as the practice of taking an annual holiday began to become more widespread.

There was a steady growth in the number of newly well-off industrialists and shopkeepers. They began to travel abroad. Thomas Cook, who had organized his first outing for a **temperance** meeting, later began to arrange excursions on a more ambitious scale, transporting parties to the continent by rail and steamship. This was the beginning of the travel agency and enabled the new middle class to explore Europe and beyond.

ACTIVITIES

1. What was life like in the late 19th century for:
   - skilled workers
   - unskilled workers
   - domestic servants
   - the middle classes?

2. a What changes were made in education?

   b Would this have improved life for the working classes? Explain your answer.

3. Why was entertainment growing in importance?

UNIT 5

Was Britain a better place to live in 1900 than in 1750?

This book describes the many changes which took place in Britain between 1750 and 1900. Were these changes for the better or the worse? This unit may help you come to a conclusion.

During this period numerous inventions had enriched the lives of rich and poor alike. Food was cheaper and more varied; entertainments were more exciting. Education was compulsory for everyone up to the age of twelve and two-thirds of the male adult population had the right to vote. Life expectancy had risen to 46 years for men and 50 years for women.

Yet there was still a long way to go. There was still little state help for ordinary people. There were no old age pensions and most working people were not insured. You simply could not afford to be off work sick or injured at work. Many people still lived on the bread-line and had no disposable income.

A better place?

Britain in 1750
- Small population; most people lived in villages.
- Most people worked on the land; some people made cloth in their own houses.
- Little machinery. Energy provided by human muscle, animals, water and wind.
- Large wealth gap between the rich and poor.
- No trade unions.
- No knowledge of germs. No antiseptics or anaesthetics.
- Only a few males could vote.
- Schools available only for the rich.

Britain in 1900
- Large population; most people lived in towns.
- Most people worked in factories. By 1900, some laws had been passed to protect workers but there was still no National Insurance.
- Factories mechanized; machines driven by steam. Electricity beginning to become important.
- Wealth gap narrower but studies showed that one-third of York and London lived in poverty.
- Trade unions important; membership increasing.
- Doctors aware that germs cause diseases. Antiseptics and anaesthetics in use.
- Most men could vote. No women could vote.
- Education compulsory and free up to the age of twelve.

SOURCE 1

From the Illustrated London News, 1897. This illustration was designed to show the changes which had taken place since 1837, the year Queen Victoria came to the throne.

SOURCE 2

What is the use of us talking about the British Empire if here, in Britain itself, there is always to be found a mass of people lacking in education, who have little chance of realising in any true sense a good social or domestic life?

Herbert Asquith, a leading Liberal politician, in 1899.

SOURCE 3

Some historians agree that people may have become better-off in terms of wages and goods, but they point to ways in which they were worse-off in terms of **quality of life**.

C. Culpin, Making Modern Britain, 1987.

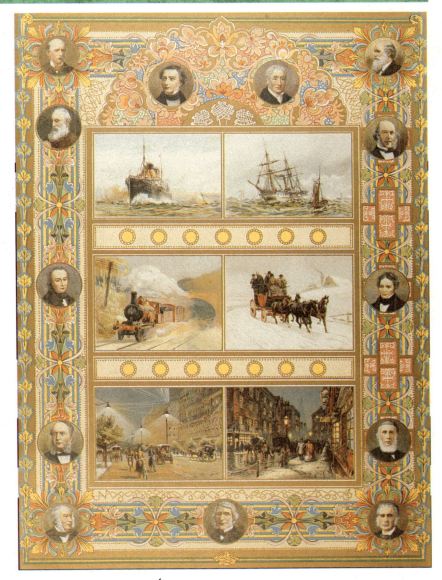

SOURCE 4

[The nineteenth century] has seen a whole cycle of changes. The steam engine locomotive by land and sea, steam applied to printing and manufacture, the electric telegraph, photography, cheap newspapers, penny postage, chloroform gas, the electric light, iron ships, revolvers of all sorts, sewing machines, omnibuses and cabs, parcel deliveries, post office savings banks, working men's clubs, people's baths and wash-houses, turkish baths, drinking fountains and a thousand minutiae of daily life, such as matches.

Frances Cobbe, looking back from 1887.

SOURCE 5

Factory workers on their way to work. This is a still from the television series, **How we used to live, 1851-1901,** broadcast by Yorkshire Television in the 1980s.

SOURCE 6

Historians disagree about the effects of industrialization in the 19th century. Some believe it brought an increase in the standard of living for working people. They argue that wages were higher, food was cheaper and there were greater job opportunities.

Another group of historians say that industrialization brought large towns, squalor, and unhealthy working conditions. They argue that a few people [the factory owners] grew rich at the expense of the workers who were not rewarded enough for their hard work.

From a modern history book, published in 1988.

ACTIVITIES

1. a What is the message being put forward in Source 1?

   b Source 1 was published to celebrate the 60th anniversary of Queen Victoria coming to the throne. How useful is it to a historian?

2. Source 5 is taken from a television programme written to show life in the last century. How reliable do you think such programmes are?

3. Source 6 says that historians disagree about the effects of industrialization. What are the two points of view? Why do you think they disagree?

4. Look back through the book, including this unit. Do you think life changed for the better between 1750 and 1900? Explain your answer.

Glossary

apprenticeship a period of time, during which a person learns a trade or craft.

artisan a skilled worker.

British Empire a number of overseas countries which were ruled by Britain. At its height, the British Empire covered one quarter of the world.

census an official count of the population, organized by the government. The first census was held in 1801 and there has been one every ten years since (with the exception of 1941).

cesspit a pit where human waste is deposited.

combine when working people, with the same interests, join together in a friendly society or trade union to support each other.

corves small baskets, used in mines, to carry coal.

factory a large building which houses machinery for making goods. Here large numbers of people work. A factory workforce has to keep regular hours. A model factory has good working conditions, setting an example for others to follow.

French Revolution In 1789, the working people of France, fed up with poor living conditions and high taxes, rebelled against King Louis XVI. In 1793 Louis was guillotined (executed) and France became a republic. The British ruling classes were terrified that the same thing would happen in Britain. They reacted by giving out heavy punishments to people who rioted or complained about their conditions.

gleaning the gathering of ears of corn left behind after a field has been harvested.

hewer a person who digs coal from a coal seam with a pick-axe and shovel.

Industrial Revolution a phrase used by historians to describe the changes which turned Britain from a rural agricultural country to an industrialized country, with steam powered factories and large cities.

Poor Laws laws which dealt with poor people. The Poor Laws were first introduced in the reign of Elizabeth I (1558-1603).

quality of life phrase used to describe how people live in terms of their living conditions, facilities for recreation, the amount of pollution etc.

reform make changes for the better.

3Rs short for reading, writing and arithmetic.

temperance abstaining from alcohol.

tied cottage cottage which goes with a person's job. If workers living in tied cottages lost their job, they also lost their home.

trade depression a period when trade slumps. It is hard to sell goods, profits fall and businesses respond by laying-off or sacking workers. Unemployment, therefore, increases at such times.

workhouse place where people went if they were out of work or unable to support themselves. During the 19th century workhouses had strict rules and a basic diet. They were often feared by working-class people.

'workshop of the world' a phrase used to describe Britain between 1850 and 1875. During this period Britain was the world's leading industrial country.

Index

agriculture   13–15
Althorp's Factory Act (1833)   15, 16
apprenticeship   22
Arkwright, Richard   6
Artisans' Dwellings Act (1875)   20

back to back housing   9, 20
Booth, Charles   23
Bournville   20
British Empire   5, 29
building standards   9, 11

Cadbury, George   20
Chadwick, Edwin   11, 18, 19
Chamberlain, Joseph   20
child labour   6, 7, 12, 13, 16
cholera   11, 18–19
Cobbett, William   7
Collieries Act (1842)   16
Co-operative Movement   21
cotton cloth   5, 6, 14

diet   11, 21, 25
disease   5, 11, 19, 29
domestic servants   25–6

education   23, 28, 29
Education Acts (1870 and 1902)   23
entertainment   26-7

factories   4, 6–8, 28, 29
Factory Acts   15–17
Fielden, John   6, 7, 15, 17

French Revolution (1789)   14
friendly societies   14

Graham's Act (1844)   17
Grand National Consolidated Trades Union (GNCTU)   14
Great Exhibition (1851)   4–5
Grey's Act (1850)   17

Hill, Octavia   20
housing   5, 20, 29

Industrial Revolution   5

laissez-faire   15, 16, 18
Lever, William   20
living conditions   5, 9, 10, 13, 18, 22–6, 29–30
Luddites   14

machines   4, 6–7, 13, 14, 16, 28
mechanization   4, 13, 14, 29
middle classes   24–6
mining villages   12
Municipal Corporations Act (1835)   18

Parliament   15, 17, 18–19. 20–2
Pasteur, Louis   19
Peabody, George   20
Poor Laws   18
population   4, 5, 29
Port Sunlight   20
public health   11

Public Health Acts (1848 and 1875)   18, 19
railways   12, 25, 26, 27
Report on the Sanitary Condition of the Labouring Class   11, 18, 19
Rowntree, Seebohm   23
Rural Rides   7

Sadler, Michael   15
Sale of Food and Drugs Act (1875)   21
Salt, Sir Titus   8, 20
Saltaire   8, 20
Shaftesbury, Earl of   15, 16
Snow, Dr John   19
steam engines   4, 6, 12
Swing Riots (1830)   13, 14

Ten Hours Movement   15
The Times   15
town councils   18, 19
trade depressions   14
trade unions   14–15, 22, 23
travel   27

Victoria, Queen   4, 29
villages   4, 12–13
voting rights   19, 29

wages   9, 13
water supply   9, 18, 29
women at work   16
woollen cloth   4, 13, 14
workhouses   23
working conditions   6–8, 14